Reflections

Seeing God through Poetry and Prose

*But we all, with open face beholding as in
a glass the glory of the Lord, are changed
into the same image from glory to glory,
even as by the Spirit of the Lord.*
2 Corinthians 3:18

Denise Elliott Patterson

First Printing, January 2012
Published and printed in the United States of America

ISBN 978-0-9837353-1-1

All Scriptures references are from the King James Version of the Holy Bible except where noted.

www.poet4God.com

Covered designed by Adams Williams with Azhea.com

Acknowledgements

As I reflect on my life I think of all those who have sown into my life to make me who I am today:

Henry Weldon Elliott and Florence Elliott, my parents who gave me life and so much more.
Weldon, Rether, Lillie, L.C., Virgie, Fred, Ronnie, Otis, Martha, Mary, Shirley, Alphonzo, Natalie and Montine – my crazy and loving siblings.

Arthur Davis, William Henry Walker, Lee Annie McNeill, Corey Thompson and Charles Young the pastors who taught me God's word and to hear God's voice for myself.

Friends and teachers from elementary school through graduate school especially those at Shaw University and Duke Fuqua School of Business

My husband, Dwayne Patterson, and my beautiful girls, Camise and Candace. Thank you for allowing me to grow on a daily basis.

Jesus Christ, my redeemer, who has given me an opportunity to reflect and share what He has revealed to me in poetry and prose.

Dedicated To My Friend Danielle Goode

God knew that man should not be alone so he created friends. I dedicate this book to my best friend, Danielle Leanne Thompson Goode (yes it's a long name for a little person). She has seen God through poetry and prose as well as tests and trials.

I meet Danielle more than twenty years ago as a freshman at Shaw University. During the first weeks of school we didn't like each other but by the last days we loved each other. During our time at Shaw U, we sang in the Gospel Choir, broke up with guys we had known for years, pledged a sorority and met our future husbands.

In November 2008 the day before her 44th birthday, Danielle was diagnosed with breast cancer. Through the entire journey she was an example of grace under pressure. She stayed positive and upbeat throughout chemo, the loss of her beautiful hair and the loss of both breasts. Her unwavering faith in Romans 8:28 should be an encouragement to anyone facing a trial in their life.

I've included in this book the poem "A Best Friend" from my book *Meditations of the Heart*. I wrote this poem to Danielle when she moved from North Carolina to Iowa. "Danielle's Psalm" is based on Psalm 91 and encourages us to know that in the storms of life (even cancer), God is our shelter.

"Before" is a poem that reminds us that no matter where the storm in life may lead us, God goes before us. He will be there to help us overcome.

Danielle's earthly ministry ended on December 20, 2010 – she is now free in Jesus Christ. The poem "She's Free" is a tribute to the life of my best friend. I will miss her more than any words can ever say.

In memory of Danielle's loving spirit, I hope this book will encourage all the readers to continue to be Christ in action.

I love you Tweety Bird!

Table of Contents

A Best Friend

How do you put into words a friendship
that has spanned the years?
How do you capture the days filled with
some laughter and some tears?
Where do you start with all the many
memories that come to your mind?
How do you express love for the best
friend and confidant anyone can find?

The confidences you shared that took
you straight from the phone to prayer.
Discussions of worries and fears
including what to do with your hair.
You've been through weddings, funerals,
childbirth and everything in between.
In the time of special events in your life,
she was always on the scene.

With each other you've shared
your family and friends without reserve.
They still loved and accepted you
even when you got on their nerves.
Through her love and friendship,
you have been blessed to be a part
of a family who has hugging arms,
big smiles and bigger hearts.

She has been your biggest cheerleader
and she has stayed on your case
to follow your dreams and not let
your talents and gifts go to waste.
You called each other with the
right scriptures at just the right time.
You have proven time and time
that this friendship is God designed.

You told each other the truth in love
even when you knew it would hurt.
So-called friends with half-truths
have about as much worth as dirt.
True friends are not interested in
pleasing the flesh but in their succeeding.
How many times over the years,
for you has your friend been interceding?

No poem could contain all the memories
or all the things you want to say.
You just know that for her always,
you will just pray, pray and then pray.
You may not be able to talk daily
but you both will keep looking above.
You will use the best communication –
prayers carried on the wings of love.

A friend loveth at all times…Proverbs 17:17

A New Life

A new life …who would have thought such love and hope could exist in those three simple words.

When I look into a baby's sweet innocent face, I see hope made flesh. Hope of parents for a life filled with love and laughter. Hope that because their child was born the world will be enriched. Hope that the family's name will continue to flourish.

As I play with a newborn's tiny fingers, I picture those hands catching a winning touchdown or making the game-winning basket in overtime. I picture strong hands that might gently hold a baby, a spouse's hand, or those of an aging parent. But most of all I picture those hands holding tightly to the hand of God.

Babies are God's way of saying the world will go on. The conception and birth of a child are two of the many miracles that He has provided. Modern medicine may think it can create or clone life but only God can give life to this small being. To create means to start with nothing … that is not the case with science. Scientists use materials that God has already provided. He alone, is the creator of life.

In Psalm 139:13b-16, the psalmist acknowledges that God had derived his conception. God had created and designed every cell in his body and knew him before he even *was*. In Isaiah 44:2 the Lord told Isaiah that He had made and formed him from the womb.

When we come into this world, not only does God give new life, He also invites us to be reborn into His family. He thinks we're so special. He desires to adopt us as His children and heirs. Take time to reflect on God's goodness and the gift He wants for us– new life in Him!

Lo, children are an heritage of the Lord: and the fruit of the womb is his reward. Psalm 127:3

Jesus answered and said unto him, Verily, verily I say unto thee, except a man be born again, he cannot see the kingdom of God. John 3:3

Be It Unto Me

What is God asking you to do? If He asked you to do it, He knows you can handle it. Those who make themselves available are given the ability. In Luke 1, God asked a teenage girl, Mary, to give birth to His son, Jesus. Mary may have had questions, but her faith was greater then her fears. She could have let the rumors of society or Joseph's doubts influence her decision. She could have let whether her parents would believe she was pregnant by the Holy Ghost impact her choice. Instead she trusted God.

God's purpose for Mary's life didn't make her boastful or prideful. There's no story in the Bible of her running around Nazareth broadcasting that she was going to give birth to God's son. You don't read about her spreading the story all over town of how an angel came to visit *her*. Mary understood she was just the vessel God had chosen to deliver the message.

God's plan was more important to her then anyone else's including her own. Mary may have wanted to enjoy her teen years prior to marriage and raising children. However, she knew God's plan for her life was better than any other plan. She accepted her purpose by stating "Lord; Be it unto me according to thy word."

It's time for you to do what God has called you to do. Don't let rumors, gossip, fear or anything else stand in your way. Today proclaim unto God "Lord, be it unto me according to thy word."

Be It unto Me

Whatever the Lord may ask of me
The above statement will be my plea.
Whatever direction God tells me to take
The above is the declaration I will make.

***And Mary said, Behold the handmaid of the Lord: be it
unto me according to thy word. Luke 1:38***

Before

Before chemo claimed your hair
God had numbered each and everyone.

Before chemo robbed your strength
God said that the weak is strong.

Before chemo took away your appetite
God said man could not live by bread alone.

When cancer tried to steal your joy
God said His joy was your strength.

When cancer tried to play with your mind
God said that you had the mind of Christ.

Your latter days will be greater than the former
God is the repairer of the breach – a restorer.

He will give you beauty for all your ashes.
and provide for those who grieve in Zion-- to bestow on
them a crown of beauty instead of ashes, the oil of
gladness instead of mourning, and a garment of praise
instead of a spirit of despair. Isaiah 61:3

Blessings to Baby

May your days be filled with butterfly kisses and your
nights as peaceful as fairy dust.
May the sound of your parents' voices fill you with
contentment and absolute trust.

May all your heart-felt wishes be granted and your dreams
soar like a kite in a breeze.
May your family embrace your presence and keep you in
prayer down on their knees.

May God's blessings follow you through eternity and your
destiny be for His glory.
May your internal beauty shine forth with kindness that's
displayed by your life story.

May the angels watch over you through this life and protect
you from all danger.
May you experience the presence of that babe who was
born long ago in a manger.

May joy brightly color your skies and raindrops be
heaven's jewels from above.
May all your days be wrapped in the folds of forgiveness
and ribbons of tender love.

May your heart be filled with laughter you're not afraid to
let the whole world hear.
May you experience the wonder of each new task and
embrace it without any fear.

May your parents nurture the gift and cherish the blessing
God has sent in you.
May God's blessings, grace, mercy and love follow you
your whole life through.

Blood of Jesus

In the Old Testament to be forgiven for sins there had to be a blood sacrifice of a blemish-free animal. We are no longer under this law because Jesus was the perfect, blemish-free sacrifice for our sins. His life on earth was sinless and He gave that life to pay our debt of sin. Jesus willingly died that we may live. His death is our way out of sin and our path into forgiveness. We can walk out of the darkness into the victorious light.

Many songs have been written about the power of Jesus' blood. One song asks, "What can make me whole again" and the answer is "nothing but the blood of Jesus." Another song says, "The blood that Jesus shed … brings me strength from day to day … it will never lose its power." It's a stain remover for one songwriter who said "it washes white as snow."

Take time to ponder anew at the blood of Jesus that was shed for you on Calvary. There are no contaminants in this blood and there's never a shortage. You don't have to pay for it and it's available to everyone. This blood was shed for the healing of the nation.

Life is in the blood. Without it flowing through our veins we could not live physically. Without the blood of Jesus flowing through our hearts we could not live eternally. It is the blood of Jesus that **B**rings **L**ife **O**ut **O**f **D**eath.

In whom we have redemption through his blood, the forgiveness of sins, according to the riches of his grace. Ephesians 1:7

Butterfly for Christ

Uniquely fashioned by the master's hand.
Images of beauty created on command.
Determined before the start of time,
And created just as God had in mind.

Viewed by many as a lost soul, a sinner.
Through Christ you became a winner.
From the cocoon of life you pushed free,
To become all that God wants you to be.

You first emerged into this life a little weak,
But the Master's guidance you began to seek.
To reach forth you had to spread your wings,
And deal with whatever each day would bring.
You grew stronger and knew it was time to fly,
And become a butterfly for Christ up in the sky.

But they that wait upon the Lord shall renew their
strength; they shall mount up with wings…Isaiah 40:31a

Cast Your Cares

Let not your heart be troubled by the tests you must face.
God will direct your every step during this Christian race.
He's not taken by surprise at the devils you have to defeat.
You are expected to conquer and put them under your feet.

Everything you endure brings you closer to the goal.
To know that Christ is the one who is in control.
You can't have pure gold without applying some fire
And without pressure, a diamond will never be acquired.

Only God can provide comfort and give your soul peace.
Seek your solace in Him to experience a sweet release.
His word will guide you through this world's minefield.
You just have to be open and willing to yield.

Never under estimate prayer in the middle of unrest.
It's in those times that God can show us His best.
The authority of Jesus' name can accomplish a great deal
For those who know His power is awesome and real.

Adversity can mold you and make rough spots smooth.
And shape you into the image of a servant God can use.
Through it all, make sure that God gets all the glory
As he put people in your path who needs to hear your story.

Don't give up –God is your helper in the time of need.
He has provided all that it will take for you to succeed.
Over 2000 years ago, He sent the answer to every crisis.
The answers in Christ – now that is truly priceless.

Casting all your cares upon him: for he careth for you.
1 Peter 5:7

Danielle's Psalm

You have your shelter; it is in the word of the Most High. His shadow covers and will protect you from the storms of life. The Holy Ghost covering will repel anything that comes against you.

He is and He will continue to be your refuge as long as you put your trust in Him. He will deliver you from every trap and snare of the enemy. He will gather you close and place you under the shield of His protection. There is no place safer than God's word and His will.

When negative reports make you weak in the knees, He will be your buckler and strong tower. You do not have to be afraid of the dark night, for you know joy comes in the morning. Satan's arrows may come from all directions as he walks around looking to destroy. Some will succumb to his deceit, but not you. You will behold them but you will be secure dwelling in the safety of God's word.

Evil will not conquer you. Tribulation will not be able to take up residence in your soul.

The angels of the Lord are busy watching over you. They will help you handle whatever comes your way. They have been charged by the Almighty to keep you safe and in perfect peace. Their hands shall guide you along the path of your trials. They will lift you up over the ditches of doubts. You will trample all obstacles under your feet as you walk the path God has destined for you with total victory. Your steps are orchestrated by the Lord.

God has sent His love to sustain you and He has promised to deliver you. He will honor you because you honor Him. He knows your name for it is written in the nail print of his palm as well as in the Book of Life. He has not forgotten you.

Whenever you call Him -, in the dawn of the morning or the midnight hour – He will answer you. It doesn't matter what comes your way, He will deliver you as He has in the past. There's no reason to believe that He would stop now. He has promised to satisfy you with long life. You will see the salvation of the Lord as you experience His never ending love.

Based On Psalm 91

Expecting

God has entrusted me with a precious seed.
I must protect it and nourish it at all cost.
It depends on me for the nutrients it receives.
Will it be junk or what benefits it the most?
For God has entrusted me with this seed.

I am in awe of this life that lives within.
Each day it grows stronger than the day before.
As it matures and prepares for life to begin,
Doubts and fears about the future attack me more.
For God has entrusted me with this seed.

I can no longer do some of the things I used to do,
Because they could hurt or destroy this budding life
That means that some friendships have to end too.
As I develop new friendships that are without strife
For God has entrusted me with this seed.

Although sometimes I get weary and tired in my body
My spirit is always rejoicing over this new life within,
It has made life richer and my past life seems shoddy.
I feel myself becoming better than I have ever been.
For God has entrusted me with this seed.

As the months go by and this life grows within
I know that I will never be able to hold it inside
It is the word of God and it will keep me from sin.
I'm pregnant with destiny which cannot be denied.
For God has entrusted me with this seed.

***Ye are of God, little children, and have overcome them:
because greater is he that is in you, than he that is in the
world. 1 John 4:4***

God Is Bigger Than Our Battles

As long as we live in this world we will face battles. They may be in our bodies, our families, our churches or our finances. Wherever they occur, they can prevent us from walking in victory and liberty.

In 2 Timothy 2:3 we are told to "endure hardness, as a good soldier of Jesus Christ." Although the battle we are fighting may be physical, a greater battle is going on in the spirit. The enemy, Satan, is trying to distract you to get your mind off Christ, to keep you from fulfilling your purpose, to derail you or to cause you to stop and give up totally.

We know that God is a deliverer and that he can deliver us from our daily battles. What about battles we see as catastrophic? Sickness, unemployment, financial ruin, death, etc. We have to know that if **God can handle the small – then he can handle it all.**

1 Samuel 17:37 reads "David said moreover, The Lord that delivered me out of the paw of the lion, and out of the paw of the bear, he will deliver me out of the hand of this Philistine …" This is David's testimony that since God had delivered him in the past He would deliver him against Goliath.

God wants to help us be victorious in our battles. Therefore, in any battle we need to let God be our commander. He will give us our appointed assignments. He will provide the armor. He will provide the weapons. He will let us know when to advance and when to retreat.

In Ephesians 6 we are told who our enemies are and what we need to wear into battle. Every area that the enemy could attack has been provided with armor for protection.

When David was going out to fight Goliath he was given Saul's armor but it didn't fit. Just like Saul's armor and weapons did not fit David, we need to communicate with the commander (God) to find out the particular weapons we need for our specific battle.

God has already told us that no weapon formed against us will prosper. So it doesn't matter what weapons your enemy has in his arsenal. It's still not enough to defeat you if you obey the orders of your commander. For David the right weapons were a sling shot and a stone. For us it may be a prayer and praise. Find out what your weapon is and use it daily with all your might.

David had to let God command his steps in several battles. In 1 Samuel 30, David's enemies had invaded Ziklag, burned the camp and taken captives, including David's wives. Overcome with emotions, David could have taken action on his own without consulting his commander. However, according to 1 Samuel 30:8: "And David inquired at the Lord, saying, shall I pursue after this troop? Shall I overtake them? And He [God] answered him, Pursue: for thou shalt overtake them, and without fail recover all." If we are lead by the voice of God in our battles and use the weapons he has provided, we too will overtake our enemies and without fail recover all.

Thou, therefore endure hardness, as a good soldier of Jesus Christ. 2 Timothy 2:3

God Is Still Good

God is still good when trails come and
battle you from every side.
God is still good when storms rage and
you're fighting against the tide.
God is still good when this earthly vessel
feels every ache and pain.
God is still good when arthritis comes
to visit with every rain.

God is still good when you and
the spirit of lack meet face to face.
God is still good when your paycheck has
vanished without a trace.
God is still good when your mate acts up
and your children rebel.
God is still good when your teen
seems to be headed for hell.

God is still good when the boss hands
you the dreaded pink slip.
God is still good when your debt
has you in a vice grip.
God is still good when you place your
love ones in the ground.
God is still good when family and
friends are no longer around.

God is still good when your purpose and
destiny seem unclear.
God is still good when God's direction and
voice is hard to hear.
God is still good when you are too
scared to step out in faith.
God is still good when your dreams and
visions blow up in your face.

God is still good when your spouse
decides they want to leave.
God is still good when that mate
forgets what it means to cleave.
God is still good when the doctor's
report and test results are bad.
God is still good when all the medical
terms are driving you mad.

God is still good when your closest
friend turns and walks away.
God is still good when no one listens
to what you have to say.
God is still good when your feelings and
emotions get involved.
God is still good when situations and
problems are unresolved.

God is still good regardless of life's problems
and sorrows.
He was good yesterday - He's good today and
he will be good tomorrow.
Take this truth and apply it to every situation,
as you should
And you too can proclaim – God is Good!
God is Good!

O taste and see that the Lord is good: blessed is the man
that trusteth in him. Psalms 34:8

God Knows

We don't know the countless hurts that you
as Pastor had to endure.
The things you and your family sacrificed
for the church to be secure.
We don't know the times you had to
minister while in physical pain.
Where you pushed your body aside and
let the Holy Ghost reign.
The days that you had to speak to your
body and take control.
Not knowing if there would be someone
you had to console.
We don't know but God, Jehovah does.

We don't know the times it took effort to
give voice to your praise.
To keep your hands lifted, your feet planted
and your heart upraised.
Times you wanted to wrap your arms
around yourself in protection.
From the fiery darts of criticism coming
from every direction.
When people you trusted and loved inflicted
the deepest hurt.
By soiling your reputation and treating
your anointing like dirt.
We don't know but God, Jehovah does.

We don't know your dreams and plans
that didn't come to fruitration.
Or the times you fell on your knees
before God in total frustration.
The times you had to submit yourself
over and over to God's will.
And obey his prompting not to fight
back but to just "keep still".

We don't know the time you spent in prayer
or all the tears you shed.
As you laid at the foot of the cross
all the hurtful things that were said.
We don't know but God, Jehovah does.

We don't know the nights you were
awaken from a sound sleep.
To call out to God on behalf of your flock,
the goats and the sheep.
The times you had to smile in order to
keep yourself from crying.
When you wished you had the luxury
and option of just resigning.
The times you wanted to throw in the towel
and give it all up.
When you no longer wanted to drink
this bitter pastoral cup.
We don't know but God, Jehovah does.

For the scripture saith, thou shalt not muzzle the ox that treadeth out the corn. And, The labourer is worthy of his reward. 1 Timothy 5:18

It's Over!

I'm finished with your promises and your lies
Whenever I'm with you part of my soul dies.
I let you control me and stayed far too long.
Several times I should have packed up and gone,
But I keep giving you another chance.
I couldn't think - my mind was in a trance.
That is no longer the case. It's over for good,
I'm kicking you out of my mental neighborhood.
You are not allowed space inside my head.
What I felt for you –thank God it's dead.
You've kept me oppressed but not anymore.
It's time for you to go, get out, and hit the door.
I know your tricks and that you'll be back,
Looking for an opportunity to attack.
When you show your face here again,
I'll be stronger than I've ever been.
I once thought you had what I craved,
But that's in the past, before I got saved.
I know that you are just part of my past
But Jesus is my true love that will last.

Brethren, I count not myself to have apprehended: but this one thing I do, forgetting those things which are behind, and reaching forth unto those things which are before, I press towards the mark for the prize of the high calling of God in Christ Jesus. Philippians 3:13-14

Lessons from a Penny

Often when I see a penny lying on the ground, I take the time to pick it up. This discarded penny may have little monetary worth to most people but there are lessons we can learn from it.

1) God is in control of whatever situation you're facing. Written on the front of that penny are the words "In God we trust." You can depend on God to see you through. All you have to do is not lean to your own understanding but to trust in the lord with all your heart.

Trust in the Lord with all thine hear; and lean not unto thine own understanding. Proverbs 3:5

2) Face the truth and be honest. Abraham Lincoln is the president on the penny and his nickname was "Honest Abe." No matter what, you can face the truth because the truth will set you free. The truth is a powerful tool that should be used continually. Honesty should be the makeup you apply daily.

And ye shall know the truth, and the truth shall make you free. John 8:32

Behold, thou desirest truth in the inward part: and in the hidden part thou shalt make me to know wisdom. Psalm 51:6

3) Small things add up. If you had saved every penny you ever got, today you would probably be a millionaire. Big

things often start from small things. Small compromises can lead to a big fall. Therefore, the little things do matter.

Better is little with righteousness than great revenues without right. Proverbs 16:8
4) There are two sides to every story. Just like the penny has two sides, a head and a tail, every situation has two sides. It's in your best interest to hear both sides of an issue before making a decision. A wise man considers the entire matter before making a decision.

And all Israel heard of the judgment which the king had judged; and they feared the king: for they saw that the wisdom of God was in him, to do judgment. 1 Kings 3:28

Ministry

It may not be behind the pulpit or in the choir stand.
It may not be preaching deliverance to the homeless man.
It may not be greeting or ushering at the church's back door
It may not be dusting the pews or sweeping up the floor.
It may not be going door-to-door and passing out tracts.
It may not be fighting the war on terrorism over in Iraq.

My ministry is found in my every day, ordinary life.
By being an honorable father or being a faithful wife.
It's teaching my children what's right from wrong.
It's exercising my faith to keep it vibrant and strong.

It's living out the gospel message each and every day.
It's listening to hear from God so I can know what to say.
It's smiling at the stranger as I pass him on the street.
It's showing the love of Christ to everyone that I meet.
It's living out my faith daily in each and every task.
It's being available to answer the call of whatever God ask.

Ministry is in the small steps that you take each day,
When you show kindness or help someone along the way.
Your ministry doesn't have to be large to have an impact
Since it's not about attention or followers you may attract.
It may be the call of mission work in a foreign land
Or the simple task of lending someone a helping hand.
Open the eyes of your heart to the awesome possibility
Of what God has for you as your specific ministry.

Take heed to thy ministry which thou hast received in the Lord, that thou fulfil it. Colossians 4:17

Mr. Clean

When it comes to cleanliness, Mr. Clean has nothing on God. He is the original spot and wrinkle remover. Ephesians 5:27 says, " That he might present it to himself a glorious church, not having spot or wrinkle, or any such thing; but that it should be holy and without blemish." Since this is what God is looking for and it's His requirement, He will make the provision.

If you desire to be clean and without spot or wrinkle, allow the word of God to wash your mind. No matter how dirty you may be based on your sins – God can make you white as snow.

If you allow God to clean you up you will have much to *GAIN*. You can be cleansed from doubt, guilt, anger and hatred. Then you can replace them with confidence, forgiveness, restoration and love.

No longer do you have to *BOUNCE* back and forth between doubt and belief. God's word is true and it works if applied. Ask and believe - you will receive.

God will arrange people and situations in your life to *TIDE* you over until you can believe for yourself. The things you thought were coincident or luck are really God's divine appointments.

As you grow and learn more about God, the stain remover – you can *SNUGGLE* into His word and receive substance.

The more time you spend being washed by the word, the clearer you will see the impact God is having on your life. Then you will be able to *SHOUT* with *JOY,* knowing that every day you are becoming cleaner and wrinkle free.

Purge me with hyssop; and I shall be clean: wash me, and I shall be whiter than snow. Psalm 51:7

My Daddy Loves Me

How many times did my Daddy tell me that he loved me? He told me all the time. However, it wasn't until I was grown and he was gone that I came to that realization.

When he left for work at the crack of dawn he was saying "I Love You." When he hustled to bring in additional income he was telling me without words how much I was loved.

He told me he loved me in the spankings I got for being disobedient. He reinforced that love with the chores I did that taught me responsibility. He proved his love with the shelter, food and clothing he provided on a daily basis.

The media sends the message that love has to be verbal for people to know how much they are loved, that if you don't hear it said enough then you can't express love or you'll have issues and you will ultimately become a victim.

The truth is I know that my daddy loved me. He didn't say it often in words, but he showed it over and over in his actions. Which one would mean the most to you – words or actions? I'll take actions! Anybody can say I love you, but actions validate the message.

The love I felt from my daddy is similar to the love that we can receive from Jesus. He may not go around telling us verbally that He loves us but He showed us that love by giving His life on the cross for our sins. God continues to show that love in our lives by His discipline and guidance found through His word.

For God so loved the world that he gave his only begotten son. John 3:16

My Favorite Toy

I grew up in a family with several siblings. Summer days were filled with farm work during the week and church on Sunday. The time found for play was precious and enjoyed tremendously. I spent countless hours enjoying a simple toy; those memories fill my heart with warmth.

This toy wasn't electronic. It didn't need batteries. It made no noise. It had no buttons to push, dials to move or any bells and whistles. Still this simple toy provided hours of fun.

If there was a group, we could all play. If there were only two of us, we could both have fun. If I was by myself I could sing about Cinderella and her fellow. I could count bubble gum, bubble gum in a dish. If you haven't guessed, this toy is the flexible and ever popular jump rope.

I can still benefit from that toy years later since the jump rope has become a staple in the world of exercise. It's inexpensive, it's easy and it's good for you. In this complex world isn't it just like God to give us something so simple that could bring us so much joy.

Our relationship with Christ can be compared to that jump rope. It's so simple but it could provide so much joy. Although it's been given to us, if we just leave it lying around and never pick it up, we will never experience all that it can do or how much we can enjoy it.

Next time you see someone playing with or working out with a jump rope, take time to remember the simple gift of salvation.

For I am not ashamed of the gospel of Christ: for it is the power of God unto salvation to every one that believeth: to the Jew first, and also the Greek.
Romans 1:16

Peace Be Still

The Wife

He loves me! He tells me so time after time.
So when he hits me, the fault has to be mine.
Only when I go too far or say the wrong thing
Is when he loses his cool and takes a full swing.
I have to be careful in what I do or what I say
For I never know when he's had a rough day.
When he sees me hurting from the pain of his fist
He wipes my tears and his lovin' is hard to resist.
When he calls me a "b" or any other such name
A response from me brings on more of the same.

Is this how Hosea treated Gomer his wayward wife?
Did he hit her in anger whenever there was strife?
Or Isaac with Rebecca when they were finally wed?
Did seeing him enter their tent fill her with dread?
As I apply more powder to hide the latest bruise,
I pray no one will guess the shame of my abuse.
If I leave him what would the church folks say?
I have no out … no choice … I just have to stay.
He will love me better, I know he will
But until that time – Peace Be Still.

The Girlfriend

My boyfriend, My boyfriend that has such a nice ring.
I may be young but I know this love is the real thing.
My boyfriend – my friends are filled with such envy
When they hear about all those gifts he buys for me.
They don't know the nice scarf with the silver specks,
Cover the marks his fingers left around my neck.
He calls me sweetie or babe when others are around,
But in privacy he calls me stupid and puts me down.

My boyfriend his smile is dazzling and his kisses are sweet
If only his smile and not his fists knocked me off my feet.
My friends tell me how lucky I am with an envious grin
I try to remember that when he's beating me yet again.
He'll stop hurting me, I know he will
But until then, Peace Be Still.

The Grandmother
The first time she pushed me it had to be an accident
To purposely hurt me couldn't be my grandbaby's intent.
Then the pushes became pinches to the back of my hand
How my own flesh can hurt me, Lord, I don't understand.

I know my steps are slow and her patience is very short
But now is when I need her assistance, love and support.
I never imagined that I would live to see this sad day
Where I pray that God would keep my grandbaby away.
Thoughts of her reaction when I don't do what she says
Bring tears to my eyes and fills my heart with dread.
She will learn to respect me, I know she will
But until that time "Peace Be Still".

The Husband
This can't be happening – men aren't domestically abused
In my heart I know that I am no matter the term that's used.
When she's in a rage, blows from her fist batters my back
When I walk away; she continues with a verbal attack.

The physical pain doesn't hurt as much as the regret
Of my wife dishonoring me and her total disrespect.
How can I tell my sons to treat their wives with care
When the daily threat of mom's violence is always there.

As Christ loved the church, I tell myself again and again
For only by me loving her that way can any of us win.
She will honor our vows one day. I know she will
But until that time "Peace Be Still.

The Answer

Your secret pain and sufferings don't have to remain
You are a victim – you are not to blame.
That person who claims to love you but hurts and abuse
Tell someone, get help, get out and cut that fool loose.

You were fashioned by God for a purpose and intent
Not to be the object of someone's abuse or verbal torment.
No one has the right to belittle or minimize your worth
God placed a great value on you even before your birth.

God is your safe refuge and deliver you, He will
Then and only then can peace truly Be Still.

And the peace of God, which passeth all understanding,
shall keep your hearts and minds through Christ Jesus.
Philippians 4:7

Potter or Clay

You are the potter, I am the clay. Mold and make me in your way. God knew us before we were formed (Isaiah 44:21 and Psalm 139:13-17)

He knows where to find every lump and blemish. As a master craftsman he knows the best technique to remove those imperfections. Would a surgeon use a butcher knife to remove a splinter? Would a carpenter use a backhoe to remove a nail? Would a farmer use an eye dropper to irrigate his crops? Would God use the wrong tool to perfect his children? No.

We have to remember how much God loves us. John 3:16 says he "so" loved the world he gave us Jesus, his only son.

Because he loves us, He will not do anything to harm us. Everything he allows in our lives is to benefit us. His mercy toward us renews every morning. Therefore, each day God looks at our situations and sees exactly what we will need. He knows how we will need to be shaped or molded to fulfill our destiny or assignment for that day.

It may be we just need to be smoothed. That feels good and everyone welcomes that stage. That's when everything appears to be going well and it's all falling into place. But on some days God can see that lump (sin, pride, lack of faith) that needs to be worked out. That section of the clay may need to be cracked and re-worked. To get an item to crack requires pressure or some type of blow. At the time, it may feel to us that the pressure or blow is coming to harm us; it's actually being applied to perfect us.

So surrender yourself to the Master and let him mold and make you, the way it needs to be done.

And we know that all things work together for good to them that love God, to them who are the called according to his purpose. Romans 8:28

The Potter and the Clay

You are the potter and I am the clay,
Mold and make me Lord in my own way.
Although I know you know what is best,
I still want to choose my trials and tests.

You are the potter and I am the clay,
In your work I want to have my say.
You gave me Godly gifts and talent,
Yet I want to decide how my time is spent.

You are the potter and I am the clay,
But I want to choose my destiny today.
You see areas in which I need to yield,
But I keep jumping off the potter's wheel.

I try to be the potter and make you the clay,
And then wonder why no results when I pray.
I'm under developed and full of imperfection,
My life seems to be going in the wrong direction.

I must realize you are the potter and I'm the clay,
Even if I don't understand why - I have to obey.
Neverthclcss, you are the potter and I am the clay,
Mold and make me Lord in your own way.

O house of Israel, cannot I do with you as this potter?
saith the LORD. Behold, as the clay is in the potter's
hand, so are ye in mine hand, O house of Israel.
Jeremiah 18:6

Psalm 100

Sing unto the Lord with joy all who dwells in this land.

Be glad to serve the Lord and come before Him with singing while clapping your hands.

Know that He is the Lord, He is king.

We didn't make ourselves it was He who did this great thing.

That makes us His people and Him our provider.

Come in His presence being thankful and in His Word be an abider.

Let your gratefulness for all His blessings be heard when you share with others His precious word.

For everything about the Lord is good.

His mercy knows no end and His truth will stand through all time just as it should.

Based on Psalm 100

Reflections

When you look in the mirror what do you see?
Is there a saint inside trying to get free?
Do you see the reflection of the Holy Ghost?
What characteristics are reflected the most?

Do you see light radiating from within,
Exposing wrong and highlighting sin?
When you look at the reflected image,
Does it cause a smile or a sad grimace?

Can you see Jesus reflected inside of you
His spirit leading in all that you do?
Or has the light grown so dark and dim
You have to wonder if you reflect Him.
What's on the inside is what we reflect.
Is it an image that Christ would respect?

There is no compromise on what's wrong,
But a stand for Christ with a voice that's strong.
If your reflection is not crystal clear
Or you see oppression, doubt and fear,
Take the mirror and don't be confused
For the Bible is the mirror to be used.

*For now we see in a mirror, dimly, but then face to face.
Now I know in part, but then I shall know just as I also
am known. 1 Corinthians 13:12*

Respecting the House of God

Too many times people look at standards in the house of God and call it condemnation. When they are reminded of those standards they see it as being judged.

When I look in the word of God, I see that God is a God of order. The creation was done in order. There was order in how God set up the world. He had order when he established the family and the church. Therefore, it stands to reason He would have order for the operation of the church. In Scripture it says, "Do everything decently and in order." Why is it we can't maintain order in the house of God when it comes to our children?

On occasions they talk louder than the pastor when he's ministering. Instead of the parent handling the situation, they look straight ahead as if ignoring the behavior will cease to disturb those trying to hear the pastor. The purpose for being at church is to hear what God is saying through the pastor. The Scripture to "make a joyful noise" was not referring to the sound of undisciplined children.

God has given parent a charge to instruct their children. Proverbs 22:6 says "Train up a child in the way he should go: and when he is old, he will not depart from it." It's up to parents to train children how to behave at church. Are children allowed to disrupt the classroom or act out at home? Their behavior may be allowed at home but this is not their house. It's the house of God and it belongs to all believers. The Bible tells us to esteem others higher than ourselves. Parents should show consideration for others even if their child's behavior is not bothering them.

Then there are those in the Church (young and old) who are constantly getting up during the service to get water, go to the bathroom or to go somewhere to do something. All that activity distracts listeners from the pastor.

When I grew up – church services were to be revered. Children were expected to be quiet while the minister was speaking, praying, etc. You were allowed to go to the bathroom only if it was an emergency. There was no constant up and down, back and forth. And if you were not doing what you were supposed to do, any adult in authority could correct that behavior. If you were a distraction the usher would escort you outside the sanctuary. This wasn't to cause embarrassment – it was to prevent the other worshippers from being distracted and missing out on their anointing, blessing or word from the Lord. The good of the whole was more important than pleasing the flesh and being concerned about hurt feelings.

Now instead of dealing with that child, parents get offended if you say anything to their out-of-control, disruptive children.

Are we judging those parents? NO! We are asking them to fulfill their God-given purpose as parents and "train" their children. Control your children – so we all can enjoy God's presence in our house of worship.

Yes, we want to be accepting of those who are "unchurched." But we need to let them know what is acceptable in the house of God. How will they ever learn if they are not taught? There is a standard of righteousness.

When I go into a sanctuary, I go with an expectancy that everything that will be ministered is from the throne of God. Therefore, I am more interested in what the pastor is saying then missing out due to a distraction not being handled or addressed. A person choosing to be offended doesn't concern me as much as that lost soul not hearing what they need to hear from God.

Throughout the Bible, God disciplined those who were not doing what they should. A word to the wise is sufficient. So, train your children and remember the Bible speaks of correction and rebuke. We chastise those we love. When we know better, we are expected to do better. So if any of this relates to you … repent and make a decision to put some things in order to respect the house of God.

But if I tarry long, that thou mayest know how thou oughtest to behave thyself in the house of God, which is the church of the living God, the pillar and ground of the truth. **1 Timothy 3:15**

Let all things be done decently and in order.
1 Corinthians 14:40

The House of the Lord

Don't you want to be in the house of the Lord?

Trials and tribulations, no place to go
True love for each other no one shows.
Family values are things of the past
Married couples wondering will it last?
There's a place where answers are found
And all your barriers can be let down.
Come on into the house of the Lord.

Jesus established His house for prayer
And you can find deliverance there.
Free to worship and to praise His name
Meet Him and you'll never be the same.
Press your way to God's consecrated hall
And be prepared to give Him your all.
Come on into the house of the Lord.

The house is where you get the word,
A place where the truth can be heard.
Where saints can come together in unity
While the anointing of God flows free.
Jesus owns this house forever more
Come join us – walk through the door.

Don't you want to be in the house of the Lord?

I was glad when they said unto me, Let us go into the house of the Lord. Psalm 122:1

Role Model

You are the biggest role model in your child's life. What they see you do is what they will do. A child is impacted more by what you do than what you say.

Our actions not only impact our children during their childhood, it also molds their behavior in their adulthood. Parents should be cautious of what we are teaching our children consciously and unconsciously.

If you gossip, spread rumors and talk about other's business you are teaching your child that it's acceptable to do those things. If you take items from work, fudge on your tax return and don't pay your tithes. You are teaching your child that it is acceptable to steal.

If you never support any missions, give to a greater cause or be of service to others. You are teaching your child that they don't have to give back and that it's acceptable to be selfish.

If you belittle your spouse and talk negatively about your pastor and your church family, you are teaching your child a lack of respect.

If you routinely break the speed limit, don't obey the instructions of those in charge and do things your way, you are teaching your child disobedience and disdain for order.

As parents we should desire that our children exceed us. We should want them to accomplish more in their lives than we did in our lives. Our heavenly Father God wants us to be the best we can be. He gave us the best He could for us to reach that goal – Jesus.

Then answered Jesus and said unto them, Verily, verily, I say unto you, The Son can do nothing of himself, but what he seeth the Father do: for what things soever he doeth, these also doeth the Son likewise. John 5:19

She's Free

On December 20, 2010 Danielle's
earthly ministry was complete,
Now she is resting in Jesus and
worshipping at her Master's feet.

Within that five feet stature the
heart of a warrior was contained.
She fought several battles daily
yet her beautiful smile remained.
The love within her was too much
 for her small body to contain
So God called her up to heaven
where it could be sustained.

The celebration and joy of this
season were unable to compare,
With the splendor she found in
the presence of God up there.
This was the greatest Christmas
that Danielle had ever known,
Because she joined Nonnie in
worshipping around the throne.

Danielle wore the titles of wife, mom,
daughter, sister and friend.
And she fulfilled each of those roles
faithfully until the very end.
Now she has exchanged all those
for a very special one,
As guardian angel to her husband,
Carlton and Justin, her son.

Her life on earth may be over but in
 heaven it has just began,
And those of us who are followers of
Christ will see her again.

Danielle has been delivered; she's been
healed and made whole,
And all heaven can rejoice and
declare that it is well with her soul!
She's free, she's free, hallelujah – Danielle's free.

***If the Son therefore shall make you free, ye shall be free
indeed. John 8:36***

Sisters

Sharing laughter
Listening to the heart
Navigating through life
Dating, marrying, burying
Wiping away tears
Shouldering burdens
Providing a haven
Standing firm in trouble
Applying tough love
Telling it like it is
Offering advice
Allowing room to grow
Supporting dreams
Crying over pain
Rejoicing in victories
Battling diseases and old age
Passing on pearls of wisdom
Cherishing each other until the end.

*As the Father hath loved me, so have I loved you:
continue ye in my love. John 15:9*

Thankful

I'm thankful for Jesus dying on the cross
Thankful He saved me when I was lost.

I'm thankful for a place to lay my head at night
Thankful that homelessness isn't my plight.

I'm thankful for living in a nation that's diverse
Where things can get better before they get worse.

I'm thankful for the truth found in God's word
Thankful for the Savior that I'm allowed to serve.

I'm thankful for the dawning of each new day
Thankful I have the choice to worship and pray.

I'm thankful for a job that provides finance
So materially my family can have a chance.

I'm thankful for grace and mercy granted to me
Thankful that the gift of salvation is still free.

In everything give thanks: for this is the will of God in Christ Jesus concerning you. 1 Thessalonians 5:18

That's It. Period.

Aren't you glad God choose the punctuation that He did when He said:

But he was wounded for our transgressions; he was bruised for our iniquities: the chastisement of our peace was upon him; and with his stripes we are healed. Isaiah 53:5

In this Scripture we are assured that regardless of the test results, the physician's report or our body's physical condition, we are in fact healed! The manifestation of that healing may not be seen physically until we are in God's presence. However, we can be free in our praise to God and our witness to others knowing that the Word is true. We have to live as if we believe it and let our body know that we don't listen to it, that we listen to the Scriptures. That's it. Period.

I can do all things through Christ which strengthen me. Philippians 4:13

No matter what challenges come our way; we can handle it with all that God has instilled in us. We have the Holy Ghost and his awesome power within us! There is nothing that comes our way that we cannot overcome. When we feel weak or begin to doubt, God's word can prop us up and encourage our soul. He will give us the strength and the ability we need to do whatever is presented for us to handle. That's it. Period.

But my God shall supply all your need according to his riches in glory by Christ Jesus. Philippians 4:19

God is going to supply all that we need. Notice in the Scripture "need" is not plural. We have only one need. That is Jesus Christ as our personal savior. If we have that relationship then we look to Him for all our needs. Matthew 6:33 says, "Seek ye first the kingdom of God, and his righteousness; and all these [other] things will be added." No matter what the demand, God has the supply. That's it. Period.

And this is the confidence we have in Him, that if we ask anything according to His will, He heareth us.
1 John 5:14

We can have God's plan of health, strength and provisions if we have Him. It is His will to provide these things. He didn't use a pause (…), or a comma (,) or a semicolon (;). There's no condition that follows that suggest these promises are based on race, sex or age. They apply to all God's children. That's it. Period. Because of that we can live our life with an exclamation of love, joy and peace.

The First Time

The first time we held you in our arms we knew
What it felt like to touch love and a miracle too.
The first time we kissed you on the check
The favor of God for you we began to seek.
The first time you slept against your daddy's chest
When only the sound of his heartbeat gave you rest.
The first time those bright eyes filled with trust
Filled with tears when discipline became a must.
From daycare to college we've watch you grow
How hard it was for all those firsts you'll never know.

The first time we put you on the bus heading off to school
It was all I could do to stay composed and not act the fool.
I wanted to race out of the yard and get ahead of that bus
Wrap you up in my arms and take you back home with us.

The first time you showed an interest in having a boyfriend
I knew a special time in our lives was coming to an end.
And that all the emotions that this life would contain
We couldn't keep you from the joys or from the pains.
The first time you drove to softball practice on your own
That was one of the hardest moments I have ever known.
I watched from inside as you backed out of the driveway
And all I could do was drop to my knees and start to pray.
The first time that you hit a homerun while up at bat
We didn't think anything could ever compare to that.
Until the day you accepted Christ as your personal savior
And we watched you walk in God's blessings and favor.

You are not afraid to speak your mind or share your heart.
You can take a lie and with spiritual truth pick it apart.
You are as beautiful on the inside as you are on the outside
Because your love for Christ you make no attempt to hide.
You are comfortable in your skin – you know who you are
And that self confidence and knowledge will take you far.

In a basketball jersey, softball uniform or a prom dress
You have accomplished much and been a great success.
That gorgeous smile will be an asset to open many a door
Whether it is in the world of sports or on the Senate floor.
Whatever career field or occupation that you decide to do
Your intellect and wisdom are what will lead you through.
Your integrity and character will lead you the right way
While you be a living example of Christianity every day.
And we will be here for you at all times,
Just like we were for all the first times.

*To everything there is a season, and a time to every
purpose under the heaven. Ecclesiastes3:1*

The Fruit of Lies

My heart was utterly broken today
And a level of trust was taken away.

I experienced betrayal's sharp pain
And "we" will never be the same.

I cried tears of bitter regret
That you had lost my respect.

It hurts to know that I was wrong
To believe our bond was strong.

It's painful to grow seeds of mistrust
Where examining every word is a must.

Instead of affecting in a positive way
You allowed others to lead you astray.

This child I loved without compromise
Has given me the rotten fruit of lies.

My innocent view has been taken away
And my heart was truly broken today.

The lip of truth shall be established forever: but a lying tongue is but for a moment. Proverbs 12:19

The Gift of Waiting

I look at you and I see that you are growing into this beautiful, image of God. I see in you all the hopes and dreams that were prayed over you while you were being carried you in the womb.

As you grow up and gain more freedom, there will be an increase chance to step into the realm of physical intimacy. Physical desire will grow if the kisses get longer and the touching more intimate. Physical desire is a normal, natural event. God knew that sexual feelings would grow as we mature especially if we love someone. He designed sex to be fun, exciting and enjoyable. But He set boundaries and expectations for this precious gift.

God designed sex as a gift between husbands and wives. Society wants us to believe just because this gift is so wonderful; anyone can open and enjoy it whenever they feel like it. That is not true. Feelings and emotions can lead you down a path that can offset what God has planned. God has great plans for your life. You are a special young person who has found the favor of God!

Realize that not having sexual relationship is a gift that you give yourself. The benefits of that gift are: no chance of sexual diseases, no fear of pregnancy, no physical and emotional scars if the relationship ends, no offsetting your destiny and God's plan, no disappointment to your parents and most of all, no compromise to your Christian walk and values.

Waiting for sex until you are married starts in your mind. Make a decision that you will not dishonor God or yourself.

What someone else wants or thinks is never more important.

Society believes that sex before marriage is no big deal and that it's hard to wait. That is not true. You can wait. You need to make waiting a deliberate, planned decision. Here are some steps to help:

1) Set up boundaries to not allow physical contact to go beyond a set, respectful point. The more that's allowed, the more it will progress until you are in a position where you are aroused. Once you are aroused you will not be able to think clearly because all you will hear is what your body is saying.

2) Don't allow yourself to be alone where you can get into intimate situations. There is safety in numbers.

3) Communicate your commitment to purity. Make sure that your significant other knows from the beginning that you will not be involved sexually until you are married.

4) Keep your goals, God's plan and destiny in mind. Spend time pursuing those goals. Don't let anything become more important. The more time you spend with God learning how He plans to use you and his plans for you, the less likely you will be to let "a moment in time" or a response to your body interfere with those plans.

The plans God has for you involve every part of you. Therefore you can't afford to give pieces of yourself away.

Premarital sex gives away pieces of your heart, soul and body to the person you are involved with sexually.

As you wait to enter into sexual intimacy – God is perfecting your mate to receive that gift. The longer you wait, the more time you have to prepare yourself and be ready to accept God's perfect gift of marriage and sex. You'll bring no past experiences, expectations or baggage to that area of your marriage.

You will be able to learn and grow with your spouse knowing that you made the best decision to wait. In waiting you will not only honor God and your future spouse but you will also honor yourself.

I beseech you therefore, brethren, by the mercies of God, that you present your bodies a living sacrifice, holy, acceptable unto God, which is your reasonable service. Romans 12:1

The Guest of Honor

The sun is no longer shining.
The band has stop playing.
The sound of laughter has ceased.
The guest of honor has gone home.

The confetti is now trash on the floor.
The candles are burned to the wick.
The flowers are wilted bouquets.
The guest of honor has gone home.

A heavy emptiness fills the room.
Lonely shadows dance on the wall.
Precious memories are packed away.
The guest of honor has gone home.

Home to a celebration that will never end.
Where God's face is the light of the sun.
Where angels sing in heavenly voices.

Where the color of darkness has no place.
Where the fragrance of prayer fills the air.
Where joy is unspeakable and full of glory.

The guest of honor is eternally home.

Let not your heart be troubled: ye believe in God, believe also in me. In my father's house there are many mansions: if it were not so, I would have told you. I go to prepare a place for you. And if I go and prepare a place for you, I will come again, and receive you unto myself, that where I am, there ye may be also. John 14:1-3

The Lord Is

The Lord is my redeemer.

The Lord is my shield.

The Lord is my glory.

The Lord is the lifter of my head.

The Lord is my refuge.

The Lord is my king forever and ever.

The Lord is my comforter in sorrows.

The Lord is my shepherd I shall not want.

The Lord is my light and my salvation whom shall I fear.

The Lord is my strength and my shield.

The Lord is my all and all.

The Lord is my light and my salvation; whom shall I fear? The Lord is the strength of my life: of whom shall I be afraid?   Psalm 27:1

The Making of a First Lady

Take a woman sold out to God whose husband
has been called to pastor a church.
A woman who is faithful, grounded in the Word
and not afraid of hard work.

When there's no one to clean the church,
staff the nursery or to get the job done,
She will step in, roll up her sleeves and
do whatever until the Lord sends someone.
She has to have the Wisdom of Solomon,
the patience of Job and a little Isaiah too,
She will need all that and more to carry
out God's purpose before she is through.

This woman has to be self-assured, confident
in who she is and where she stands.
There will be those with their own agendas
who will try to influence her plans.
She has to possess the qualities of the
Proverbs 31 lady but still know how to bend.

Because she never knows what new challenge
awaits or what test God may send.
She has to be able to stand against
unrealistic expectations and keep her integrity.
She must never forget she is to seek
approval from God and not from you or me.

The making of a First Lady is a continuous,
spiritual process that can only be done,
When this lady spends time and yields daily
to the Father, Holy Ghost and the Son.
This woman doesn't have to dress to the nines,
wear big hats or sit in the best seat.
She is dressed in the whole armor of God and
sits comfortably at the Master's feet.

She takes criticism from others as helpful
observations instead of a personal attack,
Then she looks for opportunities to show
love instead of ways to get them back.

Problems or gossip that is brought to her
attention she carries it all to the Lord.
She fasts, prays, studies and petitions
God for the answer in his Holy word.
When the wind of discontent arise and
blows throughout the congregation
She confronts the enemy with the
sword of praise without a trace of hesitation.
Praise and worship are the weapons the
First Lady uses to defeat Satan and his lies.
She stands firm on the promises of God
and nothing will make her compromise.

The qualities of a first lady as outlined
in this poem can best be used to describe,
That intelligent, beautiful woman of
God standing faithfully by the pastor's side
A First Lady exhibits all the positive traits
that a Christian should portray,
And her walk talks louder than her talk
ad she lets God have his way.

**Favor is deceitful, and beauty is vain: but a woman that
fearth the Lord, she shall be praised. Proverbs 31:30**

The Thief

I have committed an unforgivable crime
I have stolen something that was not mine.
I sneaked in using the perfect tool
My lines were polished and smooth.
The words were right and well rehearsed
I could recite them chapter and verse.
My so-called friends shared the technique
To get her mind and knock her off her feet.

Some times guilt made me want to flee
My mission to steal the gift of purity.
Too many seeds sown of disrespect
For the teachings of my youth to be kept.
I attend church to scope out my target
I'll come until my mission is met.
It only takes a visit here and there
Before she can go with me anywhere.

At the earliest chance that is provided
I say the words that get her excited.
Whispered promises touch her emotion
And saying "no" becomes a passing notion.
A few minutes of pleaser and a lifetime of shame
But in a few months I won't remember her name.
The jail of guilt tries to surround and convict me
But I don't repent for stealing her purity.
I move on to my next unsuspecting soul
And the entire scenario once again unfolds.

The thief cometh not, but for to steal, and to kill and to destroy … John 10:10a

The Treasure

In this earthen vessel lives the real treasure. The vessel may have to be broken so the real treasure can come out. Matthew 26:6-7. The treasure of oil was in the alabaster box. However, it could not be productive or used for a purpose until it was "poured out".

Our treasure is Christ living in us. No matter how the container looks physically it contains a treasure. No matter what you do to the container it still contains the treasure. Some time it takes distress, trouble or being broken for the treasure to be seen. Our goal should be to have people to see the treasure and not the container. Treasures are things that have value:

Spouses are treasures - Children are treasures

Parents are treasures - Love is a treasure

Salvation is a treasure - God's word is a treasure

God's people are treasures - Holy Spirit is a treasure

Treasures are even more precious when they are given as a gift. Jesus was a gift given and is a treasure to those who recognize and accept the value.

The earthen vessel (the body) is just the package that contains the gift. The package may have to be torn/ripped off to get to the gift. You don't care about the packing – your interest is in the gift.

It doesn't matter how pretty or fancy the package if it's empty. The packaging isn't worth much if there is nothing inside. It's not about the package (the body) but what is in the package (the spirit).

But we have this treasure in earthen vessels, that the excellency of the power may be of God, and not of us.
2 Corinthians 4:7

Through The Years of Ministry

You've gone without pay, sleep
and endured several nights without rest.
You've been criticized, lied on, pushed aside
and encountered countless tests.
You've seen the mega churches rise
and you've seen great ministries fall.
You've seen the teachings that swept
through claiming "you can have it all".
You've witnessed bold revivals that
occurred though out this great land,
As Christians around the world yielded
 to the Holy Spirit and took a stand.

You have learned to depend on God
for your provisions each day,
When the only course of action
available was to praise, trust and pray.
You realized that God had more for
you than you could have dreamed,
And for every drought in life He would
provide you a spiritual stream.

You've preached the gospel to the poor
and you've preached it to the rich,
You delivered the word of God
and weren't concern with which was which.
You laid hands on the sick, fed the hungry
and visited the ones in jail.
Letting them know that healing
and deliverance are more than fairy tales.
You preached freedom to the captives
and relief to those oppressed.
You encouraged them to seek comfort
 in Jesus and experience His sweet rest.

You've seen ministries adjust when
long-time members left the fold.
You released them in prayer knowing
they were not yours to hold.
You've seen couples divorce
and make the decision to walk away,
You've seen others fight not to become
a statistic with a decision to stay.
You've seen members graduate
and go on to receive their reward in glory,
While the legacy they left behind at
the church continues to tell their story.

The years of ministry that you have
 experienced so far has been by grace.
God is preparing you for greater things
to come before you finish this race.
Those sitting under your teachings
Wednesday & Sunday of the week,
Appreciate the reproof, correction,
and spiritual revelation that you speak.

*The spirit of the Lord is upon me, because he hath
anointed me to preach the gospel to the poor; he hath sent
me to heal the broken hearted, to preach deliverance to
the captives, and recovering of sight to the blind, to set at
liberty them that are bruised, to preach the acceptable
year of the Lord. Luke 4:18-19*

Trading Places

As I assist my aging mother into the car,
I realize that grace has brought her this far.
The crown of hair that was once her glory,
Now the strands of gray tell their own story.

Her eyes which have shed million of tears,
Has grown dim and cloudy over the years.
Those hands which were once steady and strong,
Can keep from trembling but for only so long.
The feet that once chased me through the yard,
Now find the simple task of walking to be hard.
This proud woman who once stood regal and erect
Has known some disappointments and many regret.

Once the care giver, Mom is now the one in need
And we, the children, must step up and intercede.
Although her deeds of love cannot be repaid,
There are many ways for us to come to her aide.
Handling her finances and paying her bills,
Stopping by the pharmacy to pick up her pills.
Taking time to visit her or to give her a call,
Loving her the same way she has loved us all.

*Can a woman forget her sucking child, that she should
not have compassion on the son of her womb? Yea, they
may forget, yet will I not forget thee. Isaiah 49:15*

Troubled Waters

Sometimes God has to trouble your waters to bring your blessings. It may not be until you are in a storm that you notice the shelter.

The time that you are troubled is a season. It began at an appointed time, it lasts an appointed time and it ends at an appointed time. If you get what you need (the lesson, the message, the answer, etc.) then it's finished.

Stir up – to get moving, to bring together, and to mix it up.

When you can't depend on no one else you can depend on Jesus. When no one else is there to help, Jesus is our helper in the time of need. Whether you need to be helped "in" your troubled water, "through" your troubled water or "out" of your troubled water.

He knows exactly what you need and He will get you the answers you need. View your troubled water as a time to move closer to God. When I visualize troubled water, I see action and movement. The water isn't stagnant which means things can flow when the water is disturbed. The current pushes out things that have been stationary or stale and bring in a fresh supply.

After this there was a feast of the Jews; and Jesus went up to Jerusalem. Now there is at Jerusalem by the sheep market a pool, which is called in the Hebrew tongue Bethesda, having five porches. In these lay a great multitude of impotent folk, of blind, halt, withered, waiting for the moving of the water. For an angel went down at a certain season into the pool, and troubled the water: whosoever then first after the troubling of the water stepped in was made whole of whatsoever disease he had. John 5:1-4

Waves of Life

As the waves of life wash over me,
I dig my toes into the sands of faith.
The waves retreat and then return
It takes bits of sand with it each time.
I stand firmly with my face to the Son
Waiting for God's will to be done.
God is within me and I'm able to stand
'Cause I can see his footprints in the sand.

As the waves of life wash over me,
I dig my toes into the sands of faith.
I can bask in the Son's warmth,
As it overshadows life's clouds.
The sweet breeze of contentment
Blows soothingly against my back
And takes away doubts and fears.
It refreshes my very soul.

As the waves of life wash over me,
I dig my toes into the sands of faith.
Watching the trees sway and rejoice
As the wind whisper words of praise.
The seagulls songs of love fills the air
As they glide from the sand to the sky.
My heart smiles with joy at the displays
Nature uses for worship to the creator.

*Sing unto the LORD, bless his name; shew forth his
salvation from day to day. Declare his glory among the
heathen, his wonders among all people. For the LORD is
great, and greatly to be praised: he is to be feared above
all gods. Psalm 96:2-4*

Wedding Vow

The days of thinking about only ourselves are done,
As we join our hearts together to become one.

We are happy to share this day with friends and family,
As we vow to become the couple God wants us to be.

We will do whatever it takes to do things His way,
And learn how to show honor to each other every day.

The wedding is nice but the marriage is the destination,
And it's a journey we are embracing without reservation.

As we follow God's commands and put Him in the center,
We will allow Him to guide us and to be our mentor.

He established marriage to be holy and filled with glory
And that's what we will achieve living our love story.

Charity suffereth long, and is kind; charity envieth not; charity vaunteth not itself, is not puffed up,

Doth not behave itself unseemly, seeketh not her own, is not easily provoked, thinketh no evil;

Rejoiceth not in iniquity, but rejoiceth in the truth;

Beareth all things, believeth all things, hopeth all things, endureth all things.

Charity never faileth: but whether there be prophecies, they shall fail; whether there be tongues, they shall cease; whether there be knowledge, it shall vanish away.
1Corinthians 13:4-8

What If …

What if Christians gave more thanks
then they did complaints?
Would there be more people
wanting to become saints?

What if Christians read the Bible
as faithfully as their horoscope?
Would they have a word to offer
those without any hope?

What if Christians shared more of
the gospel than they did gossip?
Would a scripture verse be shared
with others as the hottest tip?

What if Christians asked God to
change them instead of others?
Would they have more compassion
and care for one another?

What if Christians treated non-believers
the way Christ treated them?
Would they be able to lead that
lost soul in love to Him?

What if Christians talked more about
faith than they do finances?
Would they tell that businessman how
life in Christ enhances?

What if Christians spent more time in
prayer than doing their hair?
Would the homeless women realize that
someone does care?

What if Christians watch their words
more than they watched TV?
Would we then have the power needed
to set the captive free?

What if YOU made a decision to take a solid stand
To live your life completely as the Bible commands?
What if you worked on being the best Christian you can be
And extended grace to others until they are set free?

***I can do all things through Christ which strengtheneth
me. Philippians 4:13***

Why Remember?

They were stolen from the soil of their birthplace.
Hunted down like animals because of their race.
Packed like sardines in the belly of a trader's ship.
Spirits crushed and broken by the sting of a whip.

Stripped of their heritage, their name and their dignity.
Separated from their pride, their worth and their family.
They were paraded on auction blocks as property for sale
The price was the highest if you were a strong male.

Overworked, beaten and abused from morning till night.
Oppressed because the color of their skin wasn't right.
Were they not equal regardless of the shade of their skin?
Shouldn't they have been judged on the qualities within?
Why remember the past mistakes and all of the pains?
To realize no matter what God's sovereignty remains.

Sent to the back door and pushed to the back of the bus.
Expected to accept the slightest insult and not cause a fuss.
Separate entrances, water fountains and neighborhoods
The desire for equality was dismissed or misunderstood.

Portrayed by the media as lazy, inferior and mentally slow
Condemned for advocating change to society's status quo
Regardless the label, African American, colored or black,
Racial injustice is still here and it requires constant attack.
Why remember those turbulent years and unsettling times?
So you can forgive others of their past mistakes and crimes.

You are more than many different shades of your skin tone
Your many contributions to society may never be known.
You are not defined by media's portrayal of your race
In this world's history you have a significant place.

You are inventors, educators, and ministers to the loss
You are valuable and worthy of Jesus' death on the cross.

Why Remember?
To respect the past, embrace the future but live in the now,
Realizing that it's God's word that will show you how.

Why Remember?
 Because you have a Savior who died to set you free
And one body of united believers is how we must be.

***Who remembered us in our low estate: for his mercy
endureth for ever. Psalm 136:23***

Work In Progress

Filled with imperfections
Rough around the edges.
Splinters to be sanded
Nails to be hammered down.
Holes that need to be covered
I am a work in progress

My mind needs to be renewed
My tongue requires a guard
My eyes sometime covets
I am too quick to judge
I listen to gossip when I shouldn't
I'm a work in progress

I don't pray continuously
Or study the word enough
I battle my flesh daily and
Sometimes it even wins
Before I'm washed with the Word
I am a work in progress

The father is the owner
Jesus is the contractor and
The Holy Ghost is the builder
So this work is in good hands
As long as the foundation is sure
And the work continues daily.
I am a work in progress

*Being confident of this very thing, that he which hath
begun a good work in you will perform it until the day of
Jesus Christ – Philippians 1:6*

Other Books by Denise Elliott Patterson

Meditations of the Heart

Destiny through Poetry

Ministry through Poetry

Relationships through Poetry

A Butterfly for Christ

REFLECTIONS

REFLECTIONS

REFLECTIONS

REFLECTIONS

REFLECTIONS

REFLECTIONS

REFLECTIONS

REFLECTIONS

REFLECTIONS

www.ingramcontent.com/pod-product-compliance
Lightning Source LLC
Chambersburg PA
CBHW032014040426
42448CB00006B/634